NATIONAL GEOGRAPHIC KiDS

EVERYTHING
CASTLES

EVERYTHING
CASTLES

CRISPIN BOYER

With National Geographic Explorer PETER BROWN

NATIONAL GEOGRAPHIC
WASHINGTON, D.C.

CONTENTS

Mounted knights clash during a tournament. The victor may win the favor of a lady in the stands.

A noble lady is attended by her lady-in-waiting and a mythical creature in this famous French tapestry from the fifteenth century.

INTRODUCTION

PRINCESSES PEERED

FROM THEIR TOWERS. Knights jousted in their courtyards. Ruthless kings smashed their walls with fearsome siege engines. Castles set the scene for fairy tales, but the truth behind these mighty fortifications is more fascinating than fiction. These weren't just military bases or places built to intimidate rivals. Castles were homes.

Imagine if your house had a moat, secret doors, and stone walls ten feet thick. Imagine if your bedroom was dim, drafty, and maybe a little smelly. Imagine being cooped up inside your house for months as angry neighbors tried to batter down your front door.

None of these scenarios were imaginary for the lords and ladies, knights and nobles, and soldiers and servants who called castles their homes during the latter half of the Middle Ages, from A.D.1000 to A.D.1500. Let's lower the drawbridge and go behind the walls. It's time to find out EVERYTHING about castles!

EXPLORER'S CORNER

Hi! I'm Peter Brown.

I'm from Wales, which has more castles for its size than any other country, and I've visited hundreds of them since I was a kid. I've also run excavations in some castles to help visitors learn about the Middle Ages. When you see me, I'll teach you how to think like a soldier defending a castle and become an expert on castle living.

1

RISE
OF THE
CASTLES

Built between the 11th and 16th centuries, this castle on Mont St. Michel, an island in France, can only be reached by land during low tide.

WHAT IS A CASTLE?

PRETEND YOU CAN TRAVEL

800 YEARS BACK IN TIME AND ASK the people you meet to describe a castle. You'd get many answers:

"It's a symbol of my might," the king says as he sweeps his hand across a map of his realm—a map dotted with many castles.

"Maybe it's just a symbol to His Majesty," says a noble lord, while his lady shows you around their castle's feasting hall, gardens, and sleeping chambers, **"but it's our home!"**

"A home, sirrah? Well, it's a fortress, too," says one of the lord's knights as he points out the castle's many defenses—its towers, its moat, and its "murder holes" for raining arrows on enemies.

"Humph," snorts a peasant in the fields. **"A castle is just a big pain in my neck."**

A home, a fortress, a symbol—a castle was all these things in Europe during the Middle Ages, also known as the medieval period. It was a time when land was more precious than gold, and kings rewarded their supporters with pieces of the realm and noble titles. These nobles built castles and hired their own supporters, from noble knights for defense down to lowly servants who did the dirty work. No matter your rank in this "feudal" society, the castle loomed large in your life.

A massive moat surrounds England's Bodiam Castle.

WHAT ISN'T A CASTLE?

IT ISN'T JUST A FORTRESS: Fortresses might look like castles, but they're built solely for defense and lack fancy living quarters fit for lords and ladies.

Naarden

IT ISN'T A PALACE: As the popularity of castles declined in the 15th century, nobles moved into luxurious palaces that were more comfortable but not as sturdy.

Versailles

IT ISN'T A CATHEDRAL: Church leaders were powerful in the Middle Ages—as powerful as kings—and they built elaborate cathedrals made for worship, not warfare.

Notre Dame Cathedral

LORD LORE NOBLE MARRIAGES WERE ARRANGED, OFTEN WHEN THE NOBLES WERE STILL CHILDREN.

FIVE ULTIMATE CASTLES

AS IMPOSING AS THEY WERE,

CASTLES COULD ONLY DEFEND THE COUNTRYSIDE WITHIN a ten-mile radius—the distance of a day's ride by horse. That meant kings and their lords had to construct many castles to expand and watch over their realms. Thousands were built throughout Europe, where feudalism flourished, but other continents got their share of castles, too. Here are five of the most fantastic . . .

EQUATOR

GERMANY
Neuschwanstein Castle

If this hilltop castle overlooking a picturesque German village looks straight out of a fairy tale, that's the whole idea. Neuschwanstein was built centuries after the close of the Middle Ages as a romantic, fantasy-flavored reminder of the might and majesty of medieval castles.

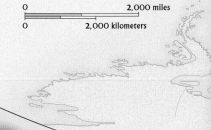

SCALE AT THE EQUATOR

0   2,000 miles

0   2,000 kilometers

ENGLAND
Tower of London

When William the Conqueror invaded England nearly a thousand years ago, he built a white tower in London to strike fear into his new subjects. Over the centuries, William's heirs expanded this keep into the world's most famous castle. It has served as a prison, a treasury—even a zoo!

SYRIA
Krak des Chevaliers

European forces occupied and fortified this Arab castle in the 12th century, during a series of holy wars between Christian knights and Muslim warriors known as the Crusades. Krak des Chevaliers had walls up to 80 feet thick and was considered impregnable.

WALES
Caerphilly Castle

The largest castle in Wales—a country bristling with ancient fortifications—Caerphilly was one of the first castles with a concentric design, meaning it had walls within walls. Turn the page to read more about this milestone in castle architecture.

JAPAN
Himeji Castle

Right when castles were falling out of fashion as fortifications in 16th-century Europe, they were undergoing a boom in Japan, where feudal warlords were battling for control of the country. Himeji is a classic Japanese castle: a seven-story, wood-and-plaster tower built on a stone foundation high on a hill, with a moat and maze-like entrance to befuddle attackers.

LORD LORE TODAY, THE RUINS OF MORE THAN 5,000 CASTLES REMAIN IN FRANCE ALONE.

THE EVOLUTION OF CASTLES

LIFE WAS NO FAIRY TALE IN NINTH-CENTURY FRANCE.

INVADERS TERRORIZED THE COUNTRYSIDE. VIKINGS SAILED SWIFT LONGBOATS up rivers to pillage villages. Fed up with these raiders, warlords built wooden forts to surround their homes and serve as havens for the local farmers. These first castles spread across Europe and evolved into the towering stone structures we know today. Here's how castles changed over their five-hundred-year reign . . .

1. The Motte-and-Bailey Castle

This early castle type looked more like a pioneer fort. A moat and timber fence enclosed a bailey—or courtyard—in which a wooden keep sat atop a artificial hill called a "motte." Lords could build motte-and-bailey castles quickly to take control of new lands.

2. The Stone Keep

Timber castles had one major flaw: attackers could burn them to the ground. In the tenth and eleventh centuries, lords constructed massive keeps with thick stone walls. Keeps took years to build and were expensive, but they were towering symbols of a lord's power.

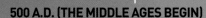

| 500 A.D. (THE MIDDLE AGES BEGIN) | 700 A.D. | 800 A.D. | 900 A.D. | 1000 A.D. |

600
Britain's legendary King Arthur builds Camelot.

800s
Motte-and-bailey castles start appearing in France.

1066
William the Conqueror invades England, building hundreds of motte-and-bailey castles as he goes.

1095
European knights travel to the Middle East to wage a series of holy wars known as the Crusades. The knights admire the concentric defenses of Muslim fortifications and bring the idea home.

KING OF THE CASTLES

When England's Edward I launched his campaign to subdue Wales in 1277, he knew castles would be his key to victory. In just 12 years, he built four of the world's most impressive castles, using concentric architecture and other defensive techniques he had seen as a warrior in the Crusades.

3. The Concentric Castle

Considered the ultimate in defensive design, a concentric castle consisted of a courtyard ringed by several stone walls, with the keep and living areas built into the towers of the inner walls. Archers and crossbowmen on these inner walls could shoot over the heads of defenders on the outer walls, doubling the castle's firepower. The only way to capture such castles was to wage long, bloody battles called sieges—or through trickery.

4. The Palace Castle

Once armies added gunpowder and cannon to their arsenals in the 14th century, castle walls didn't stand a chance. Kings moved into grand palaces and left the defense of their realms to squat, thick-walled fortresses. Palaces still featured classic castle features such as walls and towers— but only out of a sense of tradition and as a sign of noble wealth.

1100 A.D.   1200 A.D.   1300 A.D.   1400 A.D.   1500 A.D. (THE MIDDLE AGES END)

1268

Caerphilly Castle, one of the first concentric castles in Europe, is built in Wales.

1337

England and France begin the Hundred Years' War. Many castles are besieged.

1346

Cannon are first used in combat.

1348

A horrific plague known as the Black Death sweeps Europe, killing many people in castles.

1600s

Europe becomes a safer, more stable place, and cannon have made castle defenses obsolete. The age of castles draws to an end.

HOW TO BUILD A CASTLE

ELEVATION SUD

A SMALL WORKFORCE COULD BUILD

A MOTTE-AND-BAILEY CASTLE IN JUST EIGHT DAYS. THE MORE

complex stone keeps and concentric castles, however, were major construction projects, involving thousands of workers and taking years— even decades—to complete. If you were a medieval lord with the bottomless treasury needed to fund a castle's construction, you'd follow these steps to set your home in stone.

EXPLORER'S CORNER

Few castles were ever really finished. They continued to grow and adapt to new threats and purposes as they passed from owner to owner through the centuries. I noticed this evolution as I studied Whittington Castle, which was built in the dangerous border area between Wales and England sometime around 1090. The first castle here was a timber motte-and-bailey fort built to fend off Welsh raiders. But once English armies became a threat during a civil war in 1138, Whittington was fortified with a stone keep. Nearly a century later, to counter better-organized Welsh armies, Whittington was strengthened again with the addition of stone walls and round towers at its front.

After the Welsh wars ended in 1300, Whittington became a country house for its lord and lady, with better living spaces and even a relaxing garden. The water that once defended the castle was channeled to create a pleasing landscape.

1 Get a License

Any English lord who built a castle without the king's permission risked having it demolished, so he first had to request a "license to crenellate." Granting such licenses allowed the king to control how many of his nobles could build castles. He didn't want them to become too powerful, after all. Still, many English castles were illegally built without licenses.

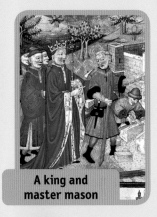

A king and master mason

2 Hire a Master Mason

Master masons were highly skilled architects who drew up a castle's plans and managed the construction project. The most famous mason of all was Master James of St. George, who built the great concentric Welsh castles for England's Edward I, the so-called king of the castles.

3 Gather the Materials

Lords needed stone and lots of it to build a castle. Stone had to be broken free—or "quarried"—from the earth and hauled to the building site, often across great distances. Castle builders didn't have tractor trailers in the Middle Ages, so they transported heavy blocks of limestone and sandstone in boats or horse-drawn wagons. Wood was needed to build scaffolding, roofs,

Floor and roof tiles made of clay

and floor supports. Iron and lead were used for nails, tools, and water pipes. Lime, sand, and water were mixed to make the mortar that held the stones together.

4 Hire the Builders

A vast cast of specialized workers made up a typical castle-construction crew. Freemasons shaped the stones into square blocks that rough masons laid to build the walls. Blacksmiths fixed the tools. Carpenters built the scaffolding. Lime-burners created the mortar. All of these workers had to

LORD LORE A COUNTESS IN THE 11TH CENTURY HAD HER CASTLE'S ARCHITECT BEHEADED SO HE COULDN'T WORK FOR HER RIVALS.

This castle-building project in France (see page 56) relies on the same muscle-powered tools used by medieval men at work. For instance, workers jog in giant circular treadmills—sort of like human-size hamster wheels—to power primitive cranes.

be paid, making castle building an expensive business. Unskilled peasants, meanwhile, might be pressed into handling most of the backbreaking heavy labor. It's no surprise that many peasants hated castles.

 Put It All Together

At first glance, a medieval building site looked like a modern construction zone. Workers wielded familiar tools: hammers, chisels, mortar trowels, and saws. They erected scaffolding alongside or inside the walls they were building. They used winches and hoists to lift heavy loads. The difference, of course, is that these tools and lifting machines were all people powered.

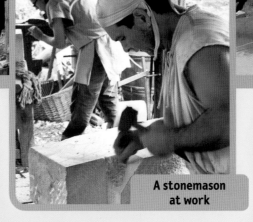
A stonemason at work

A castle wall was built like a big stone sandwich. An outer and inner layer of stone was filled with rubble and mortar. Construction had to stop once the weather grew too chilly for the mortar to set properly, so it's no surprise that a large castle could take years to build. Typically, a castle under construction grew just 10 feet in height per year.

KEEPING IT REAL

A castle just wasn't a castle unless it had . . .

A GREAT HALL: The social center of the castle. Here, the lord and lady hosted lavish feasts and conducted official business.

A WATER SUPPLY: Castles under attack wouldn't last long without a supply of fresh water from an underground well or rain-catching cisterns.

PRIVATE CHAMBERS: Castles were homes as well as military bases, so they needed comfortable sleeping chambers for the lord and lady. Most of the other residents slept in the great hall or where they worked.

AN ILLUSTRATED DIAGRAM

KEY TO THE CASTLE

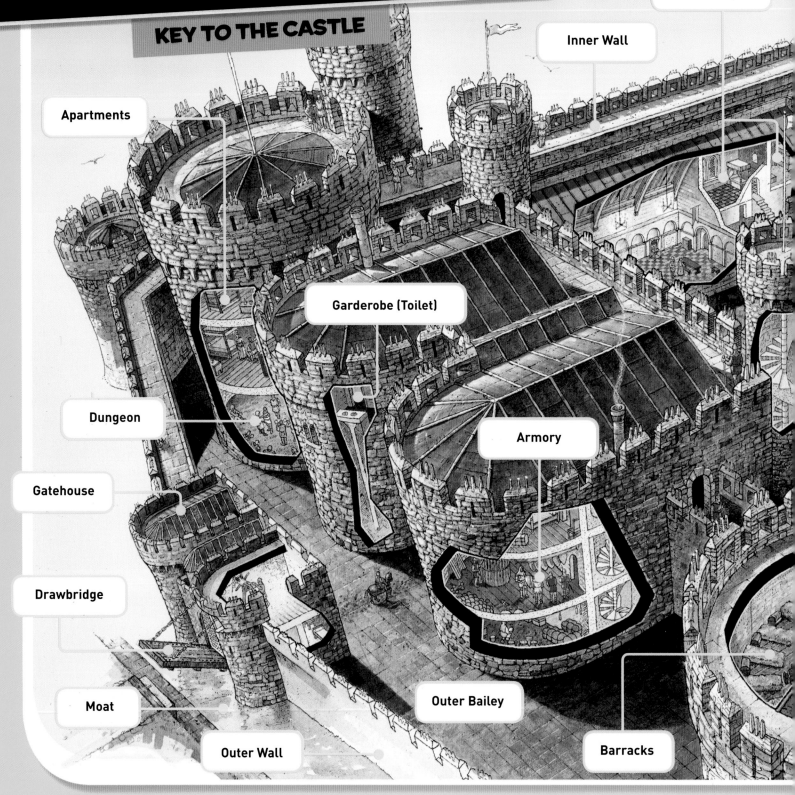

Storeroom

Lord & Lady's Chambers

Inner Wall

Apartments

Garderobe (Toilet)

Armory

Dungeon

Gatehouse

Drawbridge

Moat

Outer Bailey

Outer Wall

Barracks

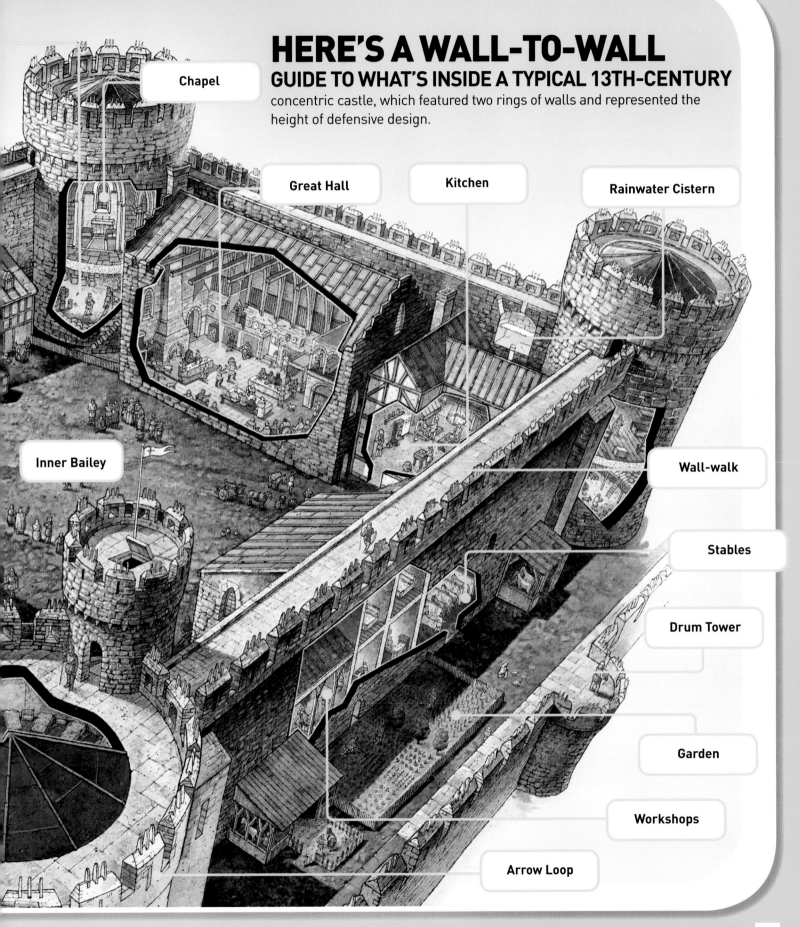

HERE'S A WALL-TO-WALL
GUIDE TO WHAT'S INSIDE A TYPICAL 13TH-CENTURY
concentric castle, which featured two rings of walls and represented the height of defensive design.

Chapel

Great Hall

Kitchen

Rainwater Cistern

Inner Bailey

Wall-walk

Stables

Drum Tower

Garden

Workshops

Arrow Loop

Castle grounds hosted rowdy festivals. The one depicted in this 16th-century painting shows how nobles and peasants alike partied hard.

2
LIVING IN CASTLES

TOURING THE CASTLE

A CASTLE COULD
BE CALM WHEN ITS LORD AND LADY WERE AWAY BUT CHAOTIC when they returned home. Let's cross the drawbridge of a typical 13th-century castle to take in the sensations of medieval living in full swing.

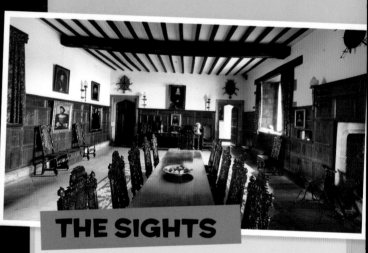

THE SIGHTS

Give your eyes a moment to adjust to the sunshine when you step from the castle's gatehouse, designed as a dark tunnel so that emerging enemies would find themselves bedazzled. Look up and you'll see walls and towers painted a brilliant white rather than the drab gray of today's castle ruins. Proud of their stone home, the lord and lady whitewashed the walls.

Inside, chamber walls are paneled with wood and hung with elaborate cloth paintings that help block chilly drafts. Although the keep's lower floors are dim and damp, the upper levels have large windows with spectacular views of the surrounding country-side. Wooden shutters hold out the cold because glass is too expensive.

LORD LORE THE HOUSEHOLD OF ENGLAND'S ALNWICK CASTLE DRANK NEARLY 28,000 GALLONS OF ALE IN A YEAR.

THE SOUNDS

Don't expect to find peace and quiet in a house full of bustling servants, rowdy knights, and noble guests with a thirst for alcoholic beverages. The great hall reverberates with revelry—from minstrel musical numbers to raucous laughter at dirty jester jokes.

A castle's courtyard is no refuge from the racket. Here you'll hear the hammering of the workshops: the blacksmith shaping horseshoes, the carpenter pounding nails, and the cooper building barrels. Wooden weapons clash as knights train in mock fights. The hunting hounds howl in their kennels. The castle's cats hiss and stalk mice.

THE SMELLS

Wherever you wander in the castle, you'll want to hold your nose. Sewage from the garderobes—or bathrooms—seeps into cesspits and the moat. Roaming livestock and the nearby horse stable make the castle's bailey smell like a petting zoo. In the great hall, diners spit bones on the floor and feed the dogs that roam from table to table. Instead of sweeping up the animal droppings and bits of food that litter the floor, servants scatter leaves and dried flowers over the whole mess. The mix of fragrant foliage and rotten food has you running for the gardens, the only sweet-smelling spot in the castle.

THE TASTES

Vegetarians are out of luck at the lord and lady's dinner, eaten at mid-morning. It's a multicourse meal of meat dishes (beef, pork, veal, and game animals such as deer and boar), pastries, cheese, and fruits, all washed down with wine and a low-alcoholic beer called small beer, which even the children drink. In the wintertime, when fresh meat is scarce, the kitchens prepare pork preserved in salt and fish and eels caught from the castle's pond.

But for a dining experience you'll never forget, attend one of the castle's supersize holiday feasts. The kitchen's cooks pull out all their culinary tricks, preparing heaping exotic dishes smothered in rich sauces and imported spices. Fancy a peacock cooked in its feathers? How about roast porpoise or fried stork? It's all on the menu.

EXPLORER'S CORNER

Although life in a castle could be hard, the servants who worked there were actually privileged members of the community. They enjoyed a better standard of living than the ordinary people who farmed the land and lived in small houses with few amenities. The servants who looked after the lord and lady's apartments were the luckiest. Their job was to keep the apartments clean, take care of the clothes, and make sure that the lord and lady had everything they needed. These servants ate better food and even got to sleep in the main apartments, where it was warmer and cozier.

But the biggest perk from castle work was the opportunity it provided a servant's kids. Boys good at fighting and riding might enter into training for knighthood, an expensive process typically only within reach of noble children. Girls in the castle had a chance to marry well—perhaps even to one of the knights!

CASTLE CHARACTERS

CASTLES WERE CROWDED, LOUD, LIVELY PLACES. AS MANY AS 70 SERVANTS, CRAFTSPEOPLE, and officials worked—and often lived— within their walls. Let's meet the most important members of the castle's cast, plus see the skills you'd need to do their jobs . . .

The Lord and Lady

This noble couple was in charge of the castle and the lands around it. It was the lord's job to protect these lands and administer his king's justice. The lady oversaw the household, including the kitchens and seamstresses who made clothing. **Job requirements:** Lords and ladies were born into the job. Noble boys inherited their titles and castles from their fathers, while noble girls were married off to other noble families to strengthen alliances

The Lady-in-Waiting

The personal companion to the lord's wife, the lady-in-waiting bathed and dressed the lady, making sure she looked suitably noble. **Job requirements:** A noble background and the right connections

The Cook

He supervised a large cooking staff—from butlers who ran the wine cellar down to young scullions who cleaned the kitchens. **Job requirements:** Knowledge of fancy recipes for holiday feasts, plus a flair for using sauces and spices to make salt-preserved dishes tastier

The Chaplain

Religion was important to medieval people—kings and peasants alike—and each castle had at least one priest to deliver daily services. Often the most educated person in the castle, the chaplain also kept the lord's books. **Job requirements:** The ability to read and write

The Blacksmith

A smith worked in a smoke-filled shop in the castle's outer bailey, where he hammered red-hot iron into horseshoes, tools, nails, hinges, weapons, armor—all the metal essentials of medieval life. **Job requirement:** Years spent as a lowly apprentice honing skills before becoming a master craftsman

The Steward

This high-ranking servant helped the lady manage the household. He also presided over the lord's criminal court and collected rents from farmers who worked the fields around the castle. **Job requirements:** Math and organizational skills

The Jester

Centuries before the invention of television, lords and ladies relied on live entertainment. The court jester—part clown, part comedian—was the star of the castle. He would crack jokes and even make fun of his noble patrons, although some jesters were whipped for going too far. **Job requirements:** A quick wit and a mastery of crude humor

DEAD-END JOBS

Pity the peasants who did this dirty work . . .

GONG FARMER: Charged with cleaning the pits beneath garderobes—the castle's toilets—the gong farmer was a medieval pooper-scooper.

SAPPER: This miner was sent to dig beneath an enemy castle's walls during sieges. Sappers were often squashed in cave-ins or cut down by castle defenders.

SERF: Forced to farm the land that surrounded a castle, a serf had to give a share of his crops to his lord and hope he had enough left over to feed his family

 **LORD LORE** THE CASTLE BARBER DID MORE THAN CUT HAIR AND SHAVE BEARDS—HE ALSO ACTED AS A DENTIST AND SURGEON.

KNIGHT LIFE

IT STARTED WITH A

CHILDHOOD FULL OF BORING CHORES AND ENDED AT AGE 21 WITH A ceremonial smack to the head that knocked some men on their tails. The road to knighthood was long and rough, but the journey was often worth the trouble. Successful knights found fortune and glory.

In times of war and peace, knights led a dangerous life. These professional warriors were charged with protecting the lord's land from invaders, leading the castle's men-at-arms during sieges, and fighting on behalf of the church. Between battles, they competed in deadly games called tournaments to sharpen their skills.

In exchange for military service, knights were granted their own lands—along with peasants to farm it—and noble titles. The mightiest knights rose to rival lords in power and property. Sir Ulrich von Liechtenstein, one of the thirteenth century's most famous knights, owned three castles.

Not just anyone could become a knight. Armor, weapons, and warhorses cost more than a typical peasant might earn in a lifetime, so knights often hailed from noble families. They started their training early in life—at the age most kids today begin first grade.

HOW TO BECOME A KNIGHT

1. Serve as a Page

A boy destined for knighthood left home when he was 7 years old to become a servant in a great lord's castle. The young page learned courtly manners, received a basic education from the chaplain, and played rough with other pages to begin building combat skills.

Good knights acted chivalrously, which meant they protected the weak, treated women with respect, served the church, and were generous and humble.

Knightly Numbers

200,000 iron rings might be woven into a single suit of chain-mail armor.

55 pounds of armor weighed down a knight on the battlefield.

45 years was the life expectancy of most knights.

40 days per year was the typical term of service a knight owed his lord.

2. Squire for a Knight

Once he turned 14, a page became a squire for a knight. He learned about armor by cleaning his master's suit—called a harness—and helping him dress for battle. He practiced fighting with swords, shields, and other medieval weaponry. Most important of all, he learned to attack from the saddle of a huge warhorse—the type of mounted combat knights were famous for. Sometimes, squires followed their knights to war and fought in real battles.

3. Get Dubbed

By age 21, a squire was ready for his dubbing ceremony. He knelt before his lord or lady and received a hard slap to help him remember his oath. (This brutal blow later evolved into a friendlier sword tap on the shoulders.) The newly dubbed knight was given the title "sir" before his name and could seek service at a lord's castle—although he often competed in a celebratory tournament first.

KNIGHT WARES

A ARMOR: Early armor was woven of metal rings that could stop sword slashes. By the 15th century, knights wore suits of steel plates that encased them in heavy metal from head to toe.

B LANCE: This long spear was a knight's weapon of choice while fighting from the saddle.

C SWORD: A sword was both a status symbol and a backup weapon for when a knight fell from his horse—which happened often in the chaos of battle.

D BATTLE-AX: This versatile weapon gave a knight options in battle—all of them brutal. Its broad blade severed limbs, while the striking edge opposite the axe crushed skulls.

LORD LORE ENGLAND'S ROYAL FAMILY STILL GRANTS KNIGHTHOOD TO ACTORS, SCIENTISTS, AND OTHER ACCOMPLISHED CITIZENS.

FUN FESTIVALS AND FAIRS

Watching tournaments wasn't the only way to unwind in the Middle Ages. Lords and ladies hosted lavish festivals on religious holidays such as Christmas and Easter. Servants and serfs were given time off to attend feasts and dances. And several times a year, traveling merchants set up trade fairs outside the castle walls to sell exotic spices, silks, soaps, and tapestries from around the world. Nobles and peasants would come to browse, catch up on gossip, or listen to minstrels sing songs of romance and adventure. Smart shoppers clutched their purses tightly; pickpockets prowled through the crowd.

TOURNAMENT!

IT'S A CLASSIC MEDIEVAL

MOMENT: TWO MOUNTED KNIGHTS IN GLEAMING ARMOR SPUR THEIR WARHORSES AT EACH OTHER

in a ferocious charge. Just before the moment of impact, they level their 12-foot lances and—crash!—the weapons splinter against shield and helm. One knight, dazed and bloodied, lands with a metallic thud in the mud as spectators erupt into wild cheers. Lucky for him, it's all just a game.

The joust, hosted in special arenas called lists within castle walls or in nearby fields, was one of the most thrilling forms of entertainment in the Middle Ages. It was part of a larger event called the tournament, which evolved from military training into a spectacle for lords, ladies, and peasants alike. Despite strict rules, tournaments were dangerous games; many knights were maimed or killed in jousts or the more chaotic melees, mock ground battles between teams of knights using blunt weapons. France's King Henry II died in a joust when a lance pierced his visor.

But success in the tournament outweighed the risks for knights, who played for keeps. A victor won the loser's armor and horse, which could be ransomed for a small fortune. Perhaps just as important, a tournament champion might win the favor of a lady in the stands.

MOST KNIGHTS IN A JOUST LIFTED THEIR HEADS AT THE LAST SECOND TO AVOID A SHOWER OF SPLINTERS IN THEIR EYE SLITS. THAT MEANT THEY WERE RIDING BLIND AT THE MOMENT OF IMPACT!

A jousting knight scored points by shattering his lance against an opponent's helmet or shield—or by knocking him off his horse.

LORD LORE ONE KNIGHT IN A 15TH-CENTURY JOUST WAS HIT SO HARD, HIS HELMET FLEW 24 FEET!

A PHOTO GALLERY

CASTLES OF MANY KINDS

NO TWO CASTLES
WERE EXACTLY ALIKE.

Depending on when, where, and why they were built, each varied in size, design, and defensive strength. Here's a gallery of wildly different castles, all of them shaped by their terrain, function, and the tastes of their builders....

Switzerland's Chillon Castle sits on a rocky island once accessible only by drawbridge.

Doonagore Castle is one of thousands of tower houses—small, single-tower castles—that dotted the countryside of sixteenth-century Ireland.

A Dutch knight built Loevestein Castle where two rivers meet—an ideal spot for defense and charging tolls.

The Crusader castle Mamure juts into the Mediterranean Sea in Turkey.

Germany's posh Burg Eltz Castle was built for comfort as well as defense. It has belonged to the same family for eight centuries.

France's Carcassonne: a fortified town

Built in the late Middle Ages, the square-shaped Spanish castle Manzanares el Real combines European and Middle Eastern architecture.

Called the "Crow Castle" for its black walls, Japan's Matsumoto Castle has a windowless secret floor for hiding defenders.

Scotland's Caerlaverock Castle has a unique triangular shape. Built on the border with England, it survived many sieges.

Established more than 900 years ago, England's Windsor Castle is still used as a royal home.

A defending knight goes on the offensive, leading a daring charge against his castle's attackers and their siege engines.

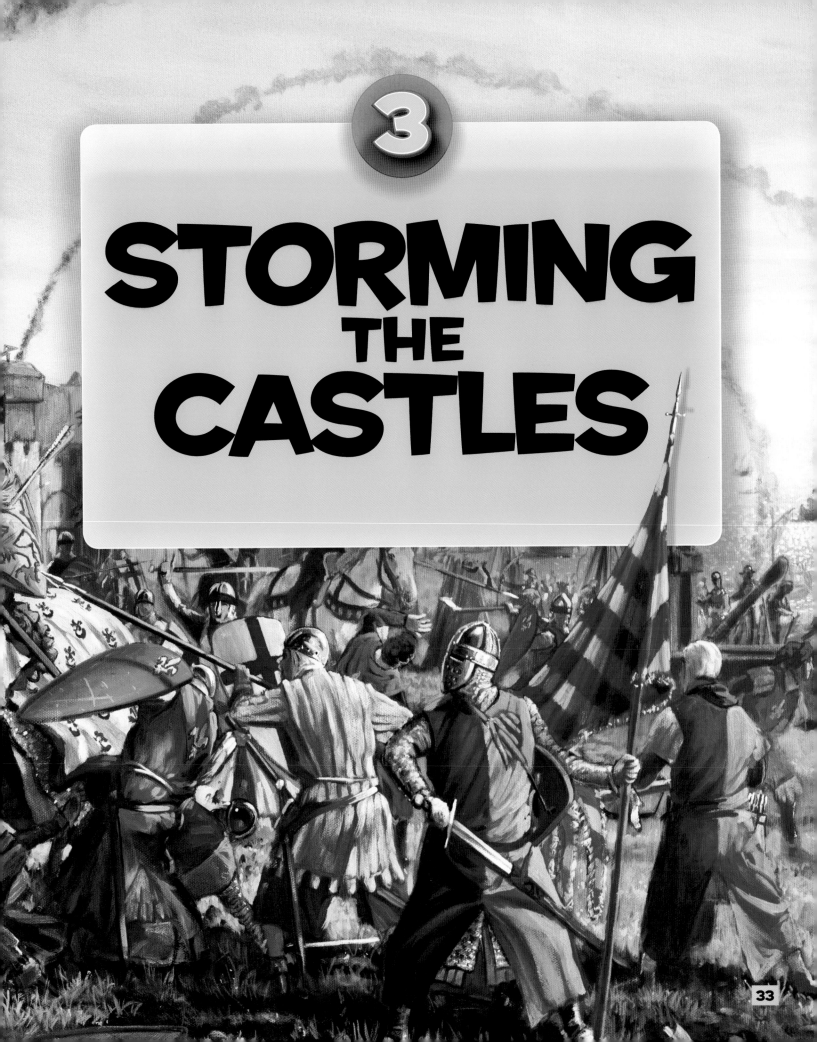

3
STORMING
THE
CASTLES

Castle defenses were great at keeping enemies out, but imagine if you were one of the people trapped inside during a siege. You might be a defending knight, a servant in the household, or even a local farmer who sought refuge. For nobles and servants alike, life under a lengthy siege could get ugly.

Although the lord or his constable, who looked after the castle in the lord's absence, would have stocked up on food and drink, it wouldn't last forever. Eventually, you'd resort to eating anything left: rats, horses, bugs, grass. The sound of your grumbling belly might be drowned out by the thud of stones or burning objects hurled over the walls by the enemy.

Besieging armies cut off access to information as well as food, and they would shout stories that no help was coming. To try to make you surrender, such tactics turned a besieged castle into a lonely, hopeless place.

DEFENDING THE CASTLE

A BOLTED FRONT DOOR AND A BIG
"BEWARE OF DRAGON" SIGN WASN'T NEARLY ENOUGH

to discourage an enemy army from attacking—or sieging—a castle in the Middle Ages, so castle architects incorporated a number of defenses into their fortresses to counter siege tactics. Here's how the more advanced castles kept enemies out.

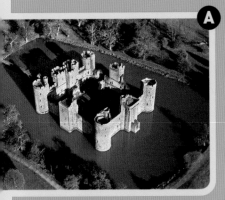

topped its walls and towers. This crenellated pattern of rectangular blocks separated by gaps gave archers an opening to fire and a place to duck behind when besiegers shot back. Defenders couldn't safely peek over the battlements to fire on enemies directly below them, so they built wooden overhanging platforms called hoardings from which they could drop rocks onto the heads of besiegers who got too close.

(C) ARROW LOOPS Crenellated battlements evolved a step further with the invention of arrow loops: vertical slits cut in the walls, through which defenders could fire arrows without exposing themselves to enemy fire. Sharpshooting enemies still bulls-eyed defenders through the arrow loops, however.

(A) MOAT Many castles were surrounded by ditches—up to 30 feet deep—that could be crossed only by a drawbridge (left), which defenders raised during sieges. Some moats were dry and filled with sharpened sticks. Others contained water diverted from nearby lakes or rivers—along with stinky sewage flushed from the castle's toilets. Moats were a castle's first line of defense. Attackers had to fill them with dirt or build bridges before they could assault the walls.

(B) CRENELLATED BATTLEMENTS A castle's most distinctive feature was the gap-toothed layout of masonry that

(D) MURAL TOWERS
Early keeps and castle walls had square towers that were vulnerable to collapse from tunnels dug by the enemy. Plus, these towers didn't provide the defenders with a clear view of the area immediately around the castle walls. New castles compensated for these glitches with round towers that were less vulnerable to tunneling and gave archers a better vantage point from which to fire upon enemies creeping alongside castle walls.

(E) GATEHOUSE A castle's front door was its weakest point. To protect it, castle designers reinforced it with a gatehouse from which guards could raise the drawbridge and lower the

"portcullis," a heavy iron-and-wood grate. Defenders could also slam shut and bar large wooden doors behind the portcullis. In some cases, a walled and gated mini-fortress called a barbican protected the gatehouse itself.

If besiegers managed to breach the gatehouse, they had to contend with the most fearsome-sounding defense of all: murder holes. These recesses pitted the vaulted ceiling above the gatehouse, letting defenders on the floor above fire arrows and dump scalding substances on attackers who breached the gate.

LORD LORE TOWER STAIRS ASCENDED CLOCKWISE TO GIVE DEFENDERS MORE ROOM TO SWING THEIR SWORDS AT UPRUSHING ATTACKERS.

SIEGE!

IT SEEMS LIKE A STUPID IDEA TO ATTACK A FORTRESS
PROTECTED BY EAGLE-EYED ARCHERS AND DEFENSIVE FEATURES CALLED MURDER HOLES,

but castle sieges were common in the Middle Ages. An ambitious lord couldn't conquer new territory unless he took control of each castle along the way. All sieges started with a blockade: The attacking force would surround the castle, making sure no one inside could escape and no one outside could sneak in supplies. Once they had the castle cut off, besiegers relied on a range of tactics to achieve victory. Here are the most common siege strategies, ranked from docile to deadly.

DEATH TOLL

	NONE	LOW

1. Negotiation

Once it had a castle surrounded, a siege army would send its herald to negotiate terms of surrender. Sometimes, a castle's lord—or constable, if the lord was away—would promise to give up if reinforcements didn't arrive soon. The surrendering garrison would be allowed to leave peacefully, although the castle's lord and lady might be held for ransom. Negotiations were not always so civilized. One king, having captured a castle's lord, ordered its defenders to surrender or he would gouge out the lord's eyes. The lord's wife opened the gates to spare her husband such a gory fate.

2. Deception

The history of siege warfare is filled with tales of castles lost to cunning tricks rather than long, bloody battles. Attackers might bribe castle guards to lower the drawbridge. One lord waited until a castle's garrison was away at a tournament. He sent his wife to distract the lone knight on duty, then captured the castle almost singlehandedly. Sometimes, besiegers would send men-at-arms disguised as merchants to the castle gates. When the starving defenders rushed out to buy supplies, the attacking army would charge in.

3. Starvation

If a blockade lasted long enough, castle defenders would run out of food and surrender. But the besieging lord had to feed his army, too—often in a hostile countryside stripped of its crops. Sieges became waiting games lasting months or years. If the attackers outlasted the defenders, they'd capture the castle intact. If the besiegers ran low on supplies or faced attack from the defender's allies, they'd need to try more drastic tactics.

FOUR FEARSOME SIEGE ENGINES

BALLISTA
This oversize crossbow launched giant arrows that skewered castle defenders.

BATTERING RAM
Slung on a wagon, this iron-tipped tree trunk bashed big holes in castle walls. Defenders would drop straw mattresses in front of the ram to absorb its blows.

MANGONEL
A basic catapult, the mangonel hurled stones heavier than a full-grown man more than 200 yards.

TREBUCHET
As many as 60 men worked this giant slingshot, which hurled massive boulders and barrels of flaming pitch the distance of three football fields.

4. Excavation

Tunneling was the easiest route into a castle—provided it didn't have a moat or was built on solid rock. Miners called sappers would scoot toward the castle beneath a protective shed. After digging their tunnel, the sappers set fire to its timber supports, causing a cave-in and collapsing the wall above. Castle defenders often set out bowls of water to detect vibrations from enemy miners. If they sensed a tunnel in the works, they'd dig their own countermine and fight the sappers in brutal subterranean battles.

5. Destruction

When all other tactics failed, attackers had no choice but to batter the castle. Catapults hurled stones that smashed walls and people. Besiegers placed ladders and rolling towers alongside the castle to storm the wall-walk. The castle garrison, meanwhile, mounted a furious defense, raining arrows and boiling water on the attackers and shoving aside siege ladders. By the time the castle fell, both sides would have suffered heavy losses.

MODERATE **HIGH** **CATASTROPHIC**

LORD LORE BESIEGERS SOMETIMES CATAPULTED BODIES, SEWAGE—EVEN SEVERED HEADS—INTO CASTLES TO SPREAD DISEASE AND TERROR.

SIEGE STORIES

WHEN ENGLAND'S KING EDWARD I

ROLLED OUT A MASSIVE TREBUCHET NAMED WARWOLF at one siege, his terrified foes surrendered at once. Edward attacked anyway, just to see Warwolf in action. Siege history is filled with such stories of ruthless kings, daring garrisons, and . . . flying pigs? See for yourself.

A Castle's Garrison Plugs a Hole

The outer walls of England's Dover Castle trembled from the impact of battering rams and stone-chucking catapults built by Prince Louis of France, who sought the English throne in 1216. But it was a mine dug by sappers that actually breached the defenses. The quick-thinking defenders blocked the hole with timbers and other debris ripped from buildings inside the castle, keeping the besiegers at bay until a truce was called.

A Constable Saves His Castle's Bacon

Surrounded for weeks by a besieging army, the English garrison of Wale's Pembroke Castle was down to its last morsels. The castle's constable, however, suspected that the besiegers were also nearly out of food. Taking a daring gamble, he slaughtered his castle's last few hogs and tossed the meat over the walls. The Welsh attackers took this wasteful act as a sign that Pembroke still had plenty of provisions—enough to outlast the siege. They called off their siege and left the castle in peace.

A King Nearly Takes It Between the Eyes

By the 13th century, the crossbow had become a crucial part of a castle's defenses. Wielded by sharpshooters atop castle towers, these spring-loaded weapons fired metal darts that punctured arrow-proof armor.

When England's King John personally led a siege against Rochester Castle in 1215, he wandered into the sights of a crossbow-wielding sniper on the castle's walls. The crossbowman asked his lord for permission to shoot the king—an act that would have undoubtedly ended the siege and saved the castle. His commander refused; killing a king with such a dishonorable weapon seemed unseemly. In the end, Rochester Castle fell to King John's forces. His first order of business after victory: hang all the castle's crossbowmen for the damage they inflicted on his army.

LORD LORE AN UNLUCKY KNIGHT WAS CRUSHED BY HIS OWN FORCE'S PROTOTYPE CATAPULT WHEN IT HURLED ITS AMMO JUST A FEW FEET.

An Unhappy Ending for Bedford Castle

Don't bother looking for England's Bedford Castle today: an enraged King Henry III wiped it from the map nearly eight centuries ago. The castle's lord was a trouble-maker who picked fights with local nobles and kidnapped one of the king's judges. Henry III summoned the might of his realm and personally led the siege.

The defenders repelled the assault for eight weeks, until the besiegers collapsed a wall of the keep with a mine. Henry III had nearly all the surviving knights and soldiers hanged outside the castle, and then ordered Bedford's demolition.

Besiegers Find a Stinky Secret Entrance

French attackers used every siege tactic in the book when they set upon the English-defended Château Gaillard in 1203. First, they blockaded the castle to starve it into submission, forcing the English to evict more than a thousand villagers. Stragglers became stranded in the no-man's land between the castle and the besieging army's lines, where they died of hunger.

After the French dug a mine to collapse a tower in the outer wall, a crafty soldier saw a way through the next line of defense: a latrine drain high up on the inner wall. He climbed through the drain, then opened the gates for the attackers. Château Gaillard finally fell to the French.

THE COLLAPSE OF CASTLES

BLOCK BUSTERS

Manning a cannon during a siege could be just as dangerous as standing in the line of fire. Under a storm of arrows from a castle's defenders, gunners had to set up their heavy iron cannon within 50 yards of the walls, then clean and cool the broiling barrels between shots. Overheated cannon would blast apart and kill their crews. Shrapnel from an exploding cannon killed Scotland's King James II during a 1460 siege.

SMOKE, TERROR, AND

THUNDEROUS NOISE ACCOMPANIED THE FIRST USE OF CANNON ON A EUROPEAN

battlefield in 1346. Wielded by the English against French forces, these primitive pieces of artillery—called bombards—caused more chaos than casualties, yet they represented the future of warfare and the beginning of the end of the age of castles.

Dangerous to wield (they could explode, pulverizing their crews), expensive to make, and difficult to man, early cannon were nevertheless highly prized for their ability to bring down castle walls with just a few volleys. Unlike catapults that launched rocks in high arcs, cannon fired stone and iron balls straight into the base of castle walls, smashing holes in them. Sappers began using gunpowder in their mining efforts, planting bombs beneath gatehouses and blowing them to bits.

It took time for castle design to catch up with advances in siege artillery. French and Italian architects caught on first in the late 15th century, lowering and reinforcing castle walls and towers to make them harder targets. Castle defenders mounted cannon on towers. Arrow loops were out; gun loops were in. Stocky, squat fortresses with thick, rounded walls reinforced with earthen embankments replaced castles. Lesser nobles couldn't afford to cannon-proof their fortress homes and fell from power.

Siege cannon reduced once impregnable castles to rubble. In the mid-17th century, the English government demolished many castles for their role in the English Civil War. Villagers picked over the ruins for stones to build their own walls, bridges, and buildings, dismantling history block by block.

Time has not been kind to most medieval castles, such as England's Corfe Castle to the left.

ONE BIG GUN

Mons Meg, a six-ton cannon that you can still see in Scotland's Edinburgh Castle today, entered service in the mid-1400s. It could fire 300-pound stones nearly two miles, creating a thunderous roar that intimidated enemies. Only used once in battle, Mons Meg was much too massive to make a practical siege weapon. It required a hundred men to move the cannon just three miles a day!

Cannon Calculations

3 ingredients went into making the gunpowder—sulfur, charcoal, and a substance called saltpeter created from manure and urine.

10 shots per hour was the rate of fire of early cannon, which had to be cooled after each shot.

50 yards was their maximum range.

100 men were needed to crew the largest cannon.

Just as castle walls were no match for cannon, 15th-century plate armor couldn't stop musket fire or longbow arrows. Castles and knights were no longer fit for the times.

LORD LORE THE FIRST CANNONS WERE ACTUALLY CRAFTED BY BELL MAKERS, WHO MOLDED THEM JUST LIKE BELLS.

CASTLE COMPARISONS

HOME SWEET CASTLE?

THE OLD SAYING

"YOUR HOME IS YOUR CASTLE" certainly held true for lords, ladies, and their children in the Middle Ages, but does it still apply today? Let's compare the kitchens, bedrooms, backyards, and more of a typical modern home with a medieval castle to see if today's accommodations are still fit for a king.

Privacy was at a premium in a crowded castle. Servants often slept where they worked or on straw mattresses in the great hall. The lord and lady were lucky enough to have their own private chambers, complete with fancy curtained beds with comfy fur blankets and feather-stuffed mattresses.

THE COST

Modern homes sell for $260,000 on average.

The massive concentric castle Caernarfon in Wales cost roughly $22 million (in today's dollars) to construct in the 13th century.

VS.

THE KITCHEN

Modern ovens are considered supersize if they can bake a 40-pound Thanksgiving turkey. Some castle kitchens had ovens large enough to roast three oxen at once! The oven at England's Bolton Castle was 14 feet in diameter.

THE BATHROOM

Forgetting to flush was not an issue when using a garde-robe, a stone seat over a shaft that emptied into the castle's moat or a latrine pit. Scratchy hay served as toilet paper.

THE YARD

Fenced in for privacy, modern backyards offer serenity. Walled-in castle courtyards, however, were full of smoky workshops, smelly animals, and bustling people.

THE DINING ROOM

Eating with your fingers is considered rude today, but forks and spoons didn't exist in a castle's great hall. The lord, lady, and their guests dug into shared dishes with greasy hands and spit bones right on the floor. Don't try that at home.

Festivals across the world keep the Middle Ages alive and kicking. This one in Italy celebrates a medieval horse race.

4

FUN
WITH
CASTLES

CASTLE
MYTHS VS. FACTS

CAN YOU GUESS WHICH
OF THESE COMMON CASTLE CONCEPTS ARE FACT AND WHICH ARE MYTH?

A People in the Middle Ages rarely bathed.

B Princesses were locked in castle towers.

C Castles had dark dungeons full of torture devices.

D Knights in shining armor slew fire-breathing dragons.

E Castle defenders poured boiling oil on besiegers.

A **FACT.** Medieval people were hardly squeaky clean. Although the lord and lady had their own bathtubs—which traveled with them from castle to castle—they bathed just a few times a month. England's King John scrubbed in his tub every two weeks. Servants and peasants washed less often.

It's not that castle residents didn't like being clean; they washed their hands before meals and even brushed their teeth. Bathing in the Middle Ages was an ordeal. Special servants called "ewerers" had to haul water from the castle's well or a nearby river to the bathtub, then heat it. Peasants washed in chilly streams or paid to use public bathhouses in villages.

B **FACT.** Medieval history is filled with tales of noble ladies held captive in towers. One 12th-century empress used ropes to escape a tower besieged by her rival. A king's daughter leapt into a frozen moat to flee her father's wrath. Despite what you read in fairy tales, a medieval lady was no damsel in distress. She often led in her husband's absence.

C **MYTH.** The word "dungeon" evolved from "donjon," the original name for towering keeps. Nobles captured in battle were held for ransom in the donjon's uppermost floors. But instead of being tortured, these very important prisoners were usually treated with respect and even allowed to roam the castle grounds. Many donjons only became dank prisons after the Middle Ages, once cannon rendered them obsolete as fortified homes.

D MYTH. Tales of ferocious dragons terrorizing the countryside originated well before the Middle Ages, all the way back to ancient China. The most famous medieval myth involves St. George, a gallant knight who saves the fearful residents of a village from a marauding dragon. Although real dragons never existed, they remain a popular myth and symbol. The country of Wales even features a dragon on its flag.

Dragons weren't the only reptiles that medieval people found fascinating. One myth holds that castle moats were filled with hungry crocodiles that would devour any attackers foolish enough to take a dip. Archaeologists, however, have found no evidence of such bloodthirsty moat dwellers.

Big Castle Breakdown

E MYTH. Cauldrons of bubbling oil upended over castle attackers are a staple of movies' sieges. In the real Middle Ages, oil derived from animal fat was much too precious to pour over the walls. Instead, defenders dumped boiling water and hot sand, which trickled into the armor of besieging knights and caused incredible discomfort.

6 portcullises were planned for the never-completed gatehouse in Wales' Caernarfon Castle.

7 years was the length of one siege at Harlech Castle in Wales, the longest siege in history.

115 feet is the height of Rochester Castle's keep, the tallest in the British Isles.

480,000 square feet of living space make up Windsor Castle. The largest home in the world, it's 200 times more sprawling than a typical house.

LORD LORE AHEAD OF ITS TIME FOR THE 12TH CENTURY, DOVER CASTLE HAD INDOOR PLUMBING IN ITS KEEP.

CASTLE PASTIMES

KIDS IN THE MIDDLE AGES
DIDN'T HAVE GAME BOYS IN THEIR POCKETS

or basketball hoops in their castle courtyards. That doesn't mean they never had any fun. Medieval children actually played many of the same games—hide-and-seek, tug-of-war, tag—that modern kids enjoy. Most medieval games have been lost in time or fallen out of fashion, but here are three oldies-but-goodies you can try today.

Como o tonzel casou con outra moller leyrou santa maria

Play Passage!

EQUIPMENT: Three dice. Simple dice games like Passage were popular in the Middle Ages, when most people couldn't read. In this game of chance, players take turns tossing three dice repeatedly until two come up as a pair. This pair is then added together. If the total equals more than ten, the player wins. If it's less than ten, the player loses and the dice pass to the next player. If the pair adds up to ten exactly, the player stays in the game but hands the dice to the next player.

Play Stoolball!

EQUIPMENT: Two stools, a tennis ball, and a paddle (optional). This two-player outdoor ball game evolved into the English sport of cricket, which inspired baseball in the United States. First, place two stools 10 to 15 feet apart. One player sits on a stool—we'll call it the home stool—and is charged with defending it from the other player, who tries to hit the home stool with the ball. The defending player can bat the ball away with his or her hands or a paddle. If the defending player hits the ball, he or she runs to the other stool and tags it, then tries to return to the home stool before the pitching player recovers the ball and throws it at the home stool. The pitching player scores a point each time he or she hits the home stool, while the defending player scores points by tagging the other stool.

Grown-up games: Knights and nobles played chess—not only for fun but to sharpen their strategic skills for battle.

LORD LORE A CHAOTIC PRECURSOR TO SOCCER CALLED CAMPBALL OFTEN ENDED WITH PLAYERS BEATEN AND BLOODIED.

Nobles preferred lofty and expensive pastimes, such as training pet falcons to hunt.

SUNRISE: Eat breakfast, attend Mass in the chapel

9 a.m.: Hold court, collect rents from peasants

11 a.m.: Eat a large meal and listen to minstrels in the great hall

2 p.m.: Enjoy an afternoon hunt on the castle grounds

SUNSET: Eat dinner in the great hall, retire to private chambers

Play Blind Man's Bluff!

EQUIPMENT: A blindfold. Here's an ancient variation of tag that has stood the test of time. One player is chosen as "it" and dons a blindfold. Everyone else surrounds this player and spins him or her in a few circles. Once the blindfolded player is disoriented, the other players dart in and tag him or her. The blindfolded player tries to grab the other players and guess the identity of anyone who gets snagged. If the blindfolded player guesses correctly, his or her target becomes "it." That player puts on the blindfold and the next round begins.

THE ART OF HERALDRY

The coat of arms of England's Richard I featured three lions. A warrior king in the Crusades, he was known as Richard the Lionheart.

IMAGINE WATCHING A FOOTBALL

GAME IN WHICH BOTH TEAMS' PLAYERS WEAR IDENTICAL HELMETS AND JERSEYS. You wouldn't be able to tell one team from the other, and neither would the players. They'd end up bumbling around the field, unable to help their teammates. Medieval knights faced this same problem in the 12th century. Helmets and armor hid faces and forms, making it hard to identify friends and foes in battle. Tournament competitors realized they needed identifying symbols so crowds could follow their exploits. Knights began decorating their tunics, shields, saddle blankets, and pennants with shapes, plants, birds, beasts—meaningful images that symbolized personal feats or family backgrounds. These designs became each knight's "coat of arms," and the art of heraldry was born.

Soon, everyone from nobles to priests to entire cities began identifying themselves with unique coats of arms, and it was the job of experts called heralds to interpret these designs and know the rules for their use. Coats of arms passed from fathers to sons and daughters. You can still see them used today by families, businesses, and countries.

COAT COMBINATIONS

When two noble families joined through marriage or alliance, they combined their coats of arms on a single shield by dividing it into quarters. Centuries of marriage could lead to garish shields crowded with dozens of symbols.

LORD LORE SOME HISTORIANS BELIEVE VANITY, RATHER THAN BATTLEFIELD NECESSITY, GAVE RISE TO HERALDRY.

CREATE YOUR OWN COAT OF ARMS

It took the combined expertise of an artist and a herald to create a coat of arms in the Middle Ages. Today, you just need a poster board, scissors, and some colored markers. Follow these steps and simplified heraldic rules to wield a shield that suits your personality.

Trace Your Field

Trace a basic shield shape like the one shown here on a piece of poster board. This will be your shield's "field" on which you'll draw and color your coat of arms. Don't cut it out until you've finished your design.

Give It Shape

Decide if you want your shield to have an "ordinary." These are simple shapes that symbolize a particular principle. Here are some to choose from.

CHIEF Authority | **BEND** Defense | **CANTON** Honor | **CHEVRON** Protection | **PILE** Great military strength

Choose Your Charge

It's time to "charge" your coat of arms. Charges are the various beasts, beings, and inanimate objects that make your shield look so smashing. Here are a few examples, along with their meanings. Choose one or more and doodle away.

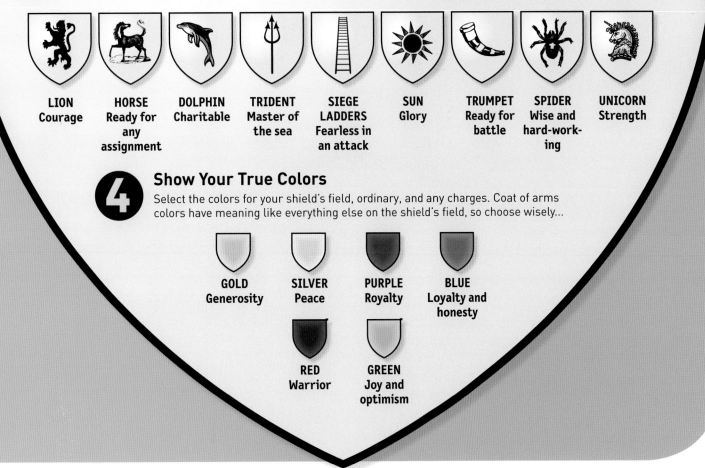

LION Courage | **HORSE** Ready for any assignment | **DOLPHIN** Charitable | **TRIDENT** Master of the sea | **SIEGE LADDERS** Fearless in an attack | **SUN** Glory | **TRUMPET** Ready for battle | **SPIDER** Wise and hard-working | **UNICORN** Strength

Show Your True Colors

Select the colors for your shield's field, ordinary, and any charges. Coat of arms colors have meaning like everything else on the shield's field, so choose wisely...

GOLD Generosity | **SILVER** Peace | **PURPLE** Royalty | **BLUE** Loyalty and honesty

RED Warrior | **GREEN** Joy and optimism

POP CULTURE CASTLES

MATCH THE
REAL-WORLD CASTLE ON THE LEFT with the mythical or make-believe location that's associated with it on the right.

A

B

❶ Alnwick Castle

This sprawling castle, still used as a royal home in England, was built late in the 11th century and was significantly fortified throughout the Middle Ages. It survived several sieges and stands today as a popular tourist site and movie backdrop.

❷ Bran Castle

Perched atop a windswept crag in Romania, Bran Castle served as the headquarters for Vlad Tepes, a ruthless 15th-century prince who waged war against the Turks. Infamous for his cruelty, Vlad tortured his enemies to death by impaling them on long stakes. It earned him the nickname "Vlad the Impaler."

C

❸ Neuschwanstein Castle

Featured as one of our "five ultimate castles" back on page 12, Neuschwanstein Castle is a 19th-century palace that rekindles the fairy-tale flavor of the Middle Ages.

❹ Cadbury Castle

It doesn't look like much today—just a grassy hill in the English countryside. But archaeologists have found evidence that a massive timber castle sat here in the early Middle Ages. Local legend has it that a famous king once lived in Cadbury Castle.

D

Sleeping Beauty Castle

This iconic castle at California's Disneyland theme park incorporates familiar Middle Ages defenses—a moat, a working drawbridge, and fanciful towers—into its design. The inside of the castle is anything but medieval, however. Among other things, it houses a beauty salon.

King Arthur's Camelot

Tales of King Arthur, who rose to power after plucking the sword Excalibur from a stone, have been told since the early Middle Ages. It's a story rich with magic, romance, a gallant quest for the Holy Grail, and chivalrous knights who met at a round table in Arthur's gleaming castle, Camelot.

Hogwarts

The most common setting in the Harry Potter books and films, this famous school of witchcraft and wizardry is depicted as a massive Scottish castle complete with a great hall, gardens, ghosts, and its own Quidditch pitch. Although it is surrounded by walls and towers, Hogwarts relies on defensive spells to protect its students and hide it from the prying eyes of non-magical Muggles.

Count Dracula's Castle

Home to the neck-biting, blood-sucking vampire of Bram Stoker's 1897 novel, Dracula's Castle is described as a scary, rundown fortress high in the mountains of Romania.

CHOOSE YOUR CASTLE!

Answer these four questions to see which real-world castle suits your style.

1 **What type of terrain would you like your castle to sit on or near?**
A. A moat or lake
B. A hill or crag
C. Near a river or other important route
D. In a forest

2 **What kind of design would you prefer for your castle?**
A. A walled-in courtyard
B. A concentric design
C. A stone keep
D. Something out of a fairy tale

3 **You want this castle to . . .**
A. . . . serve as a status symbol
B. . . . provide the ultimate in protection
C. . . . hold a key strategic position
D. . . . offer unparalleled luxury

4 **When would you like your castle to have been built?**
A. 14th century
B. 13th century
C. 12th century
D. 20th century

IF YOU SCORED MOSTLY:

A: You'd prefer living in Bodiam, a stunning storybook castle in England with perfectly symmetrical walls. It sits in the middle of an enormous moat, which reflects the castle's walls and creates the illusion that Bodiam is larger than it actually is.

B: You'd want to live in Harlech Castle, one of the great concentric castles built during the reign of England's King Edward I. It sits atop a cliff overlooking a bay and has an impenetrable gatehouse on its landward side.

C: You'd like to live in Rochester Castle, a towering stone keep that guards a vital road leading to London. Rochester has four floors and a comfortable, richly decorated great hall.

D: You'd make your home at California's Hearst Castle, built for American multimillionaire William Randolph Hearst in the 1920s. Despite modern touches such as swimming pools and a movie theater, much of this mansion's design was inspired by castle architecture.

PHOTO FINISH

THE INCREDIBLE KRAK
BY PETER BROWN

PERCHED AT THE END OF
A HIGH RIDGE WHERE IT DOMINATES

the landscape, Syria's Krak des Chevaliers was the greatest of all the Crusader castles. The Order of Knights known as the Hospitallers rebuilt an earlier castle on the site after 1142, and even the great Muslim leader Saladin realized it was unassailable when he visited later. Following an earthquake in 1202, this concentric castle was rebuilt once again in the form we see today.

The Krak was a self-contained community where 2,000 soldiers and their horses could hold out against a siege for years. It contained vast storage chambers for grain—and even a windmill to grind corn. A deep well and rain cisterns supplied ample water.

In its heyday, the castle was never seriously tested by a siege. That changed in 1271, when Sultan Baybars decided to attack. By then, the Crusaders had fewer resources to defend the castle. Rather than trying to starve out the garrison, the sultan chose to sap the walls and batter them with siege engines (the Muslim engineers were very skilled at these tactics). Despite the massive defenses and the efforts of the defenders, the miners brought down one of the towers, allowing them to get inside the outer walls as the garrison retreated to the center. The defenders began peace talks once they saw the end was near. Or maybe they were motivated by another reason—it is said the Muslims produced a forged letter from the Hospitallers' commander ordering knights to surrender.

Once seemingly impenetrable, the castle fell after only 35 days to a combination of low manpower, dwindling supplies, mining, siege engines, and perhaps even trickery. The technology of attack had overtaken the technology of defense. The defeated knights were allowed to leave safely, and the Muslim army assumed control of the incredible Krak.

AFTERWORD

CASTLES WERE BUILT
TO LAST, BUT EVEN THE THICKEST

WALLS and mightiest keeps had their limits. Consider the sad fate of England's Corfe Castle. Begun as a keep on a hill in the late 11th century, Corfe evolved into a fine concentric castle that survived sieges and stood strong until 1646. That's when England's government ordered the castle "slighted"—or demolished—for its role in the English Civil War. The proud castle was being punished for serving the war's losing side.

Corfe didn't stand a chance. Its towers were undermined and tipped. Gunpowder charges blew its walls to smithereens. Many other castles were slighted using similar systematic methods. Rain, wind, and scavenging villagers further eroded their walls and towers over the centuries. The fact that so many castles still stand today—even as crumbling ruins—is a testament to their builders' skills, but archaeologists wish they had more pristine structures to study.

And they're doing something about it. In a rock quarry deep in a French forest, archaeologists and craftsmen are building their own full-size 13th-century castle using nothing but medieval methods of construction—no bulldozers, no cranes, no power tools. Called The Guédelon Adventure, the castle is nearly half finished (with a similar castle-building project just starting in Arkansas). Thousands of visitors tour Guédelon's site each year to see firsthand how stone blocks were cut and laid, how mortar was made, how heavy loads were lifted using nothing but muscle power.

The Guédelon Adventure's master mason and his crew of workers are basing their building techniques on medieval financial records, ancient illustrations, accounts from Middle Ages chroniclers, and castle ruins today. The result is a hands-on history lesson for archaeologists and visitors alike.

Now that you've read *Everything Castles*, you already know how castles were constructed. You'd recognize the tools and building techniques used at Guédelon. You'd be able to identify the nearly finished great hall, the inner bailey, and the beginnings of towers and walls. Castles like Corfe may be gone, but the Guédelon project is helping make sure they're not forgotten. Now you've become an expert on everything castles, and you can share your knowledge of these awesome monuments to the Middle Ages.

Begun in 1997, the Guédelon building project will run until 2025, when the finished castle will look like the computer-rendered model to the left.

Renaissance fairs offer a fun way to relive the Middle Ages. Keep an eye out for one near you.

AN **INTERACTIVE GLOSSARY**

The immense castle of Mont St. Michel in France started out as a small church built in the 8th century.

THESE WORDS ARE

COMMONLY USED among archaeologists who study castles. Use the glossary to learn what each word means and visit its page numbers to see the word used in context. Then test your noble knowledge!

Chaplain
(PAGES 24-25)
The castle's priest, charged with looking after the spiritual health of the lord and lady

A chaplain's duties included __.
a. delivering daily church services
b. teaching pages to read and write
c. keeping the lord's books
d. all of the above

Coat of arms
(PAGES 50-51)
A colored shield covered with heraldic symbols and shapes that represent a knight or noble family

Why did coats of arms develop?
a. to serve as a decoration in a castle's great hall
b. to give heralds a job
c. to help knights recognize each other in battles and tournaments
d. all of the above

Concentric castle
(PAGES 14-15)
An advanced type of castle with inner and outer walls that protect a central courtyard

Concentric castles are considered the ultimate in defensive design because __.
a. archers on the inner walls could shoot over the heads of their allies on the lower outer walls
b. their walls were perfectly symmetrical
c. attackers were intimidated by their size
d. all of the above

Crenellations
(PAGES 34-35)
The distinctive gap-toothed pattern of blocks along the top of a castle's walls and towers

What was the purpose of crenellations?
a. to prevent attackers from placing ladders next to the castle
b. to give guards a place to sit while taking a break
c. to give castles their classic look
d. to provide archers with cover and openings from which to shoot

Donjon
(PAGES 46-47)
The original name for a castle's keep

The earliest donjons were made of __.
a. stone
b. wood
c. cement
d. brick

Feudal system
(PAGES 10-11)
A Middle Ages social arrangement in which a king divides his realm among noble supporters in exchange for an oath of loyalty. These supporters often split their holdings among their own supporters.

Which of these duties were required under feudal law?
a. a lord had to supply knights to his king when required
b. a knight owed 40 days of military service to his lord
c. a peasant had to give a percentage of his crop to his lord
d. all of the above

Garderobe
(PAGES 24-25, 42-43)
A medieval bathroom, usually nothing fancier than a hole cut through a stone bench in the castle wall overhanging the moat or a latrine pit

The person tasked with cleaning the pit below a garderobe was called a __.
a. gong farmer
b. sapper
c. page
d. serf

Jester
(PAGES 24-25)
The castle's comedian. His job is to entertain the lord, lady, and their guests.

A good jester knows how to __.
a. juggle
b. poke fun at his lord and lady
c. tell crude jokes
d. all of the above

Motte-and-Bailey castle
(PAGES 14-15)
The earliest type of castle, consisting of a courtyard encircled by a timber fence and a man-made hill on which sat a donjon

What advantage does a motte-and-bailey castle have over other types of castles?
a. it's fireproof
b. it can be built quickly
c. it has indoor plumbing
d. all of the above

Murder holes
(PAGES 34-35)
Holes in the ceiling above a castle's gatehouse. Defenders above the holes can fire arrows at intruders below

Besides arrows, what other objects or substances did castle defenders drop through murder holes?
a. boiling water
b. scalding sand
c. water to extinguish fires set by intruders
d. all of the above

Serf
(PAGES 24-25)
A common peasant forced to farm the land around the castle

Name one perk of serf life?
a. serfs could attend festivals and shop at markets near the castle
b. serfs could leave the land whenever they wished
c. serfs could grind their grain in the lord's mill for free
d. serfs could keep everything they grew for their families

Siege
(PAGES 34-35, 36-37, 38-39)
An attack on a castle, with the goal of capturing it

Which of these is not an effective siege tactic?
a. blockading the castle's supplies
b. digging under the castle's walls
c. setting fire to the surrounding countryside
d. launching dead animals into the castle

Squire
(PAGES 26-27)
A young man training for knighthood. He doesn't become a knight until his dubbing ceremony.

Which of these people could dub a squire, thus granting him knighthood?
a. his master knight
b. his lord or lady
c. his king
d. all of the above

Trebuchet
(PAGES 36-37)
An advanced weight-driven siege engine that hurls massive missiles at castle walls

Which of these was used as trebuchet ammunition?
a. flaming barrels
b. dead bodies
c. manure
d. all of the above

ANSWERS: Chaplain: d; Coat of arms: c; Concentric castle: a; Crenellations: d; Donjon: b; Feudal system: d; Garderobe: a; Jester: d; Motte-and-Bailey Castle: d; Murder holes: b; Serf: a; Siege: c; Squire: d; Trebuchet: d.

FIND OUT MORE

Extend your stay in the medieval world with these websites, games, and books . . .

CASTLE SITES

www.castlesontheweb.com
A massive collection of castle profiles, photos, facts, and more

www.castles-of-britain.com
Click the Castle Learning Center link for fun stories about castle life.

www.guedelon.fr
See photos and videos of a castle being built using medieval tools in France.

www.channel4.com/history/microsites/H/history/guide12/index.html
A time-traveler's guide to the Middle Ages

CASTLE GAMES

The Sims Medieval
Build your own kingdom and rule it wisely in this medieval installment of the popular PC series.

Treb Challenge
Visit www.globalspec.com/trebuchet to play a free, block-busting trebuchet simulator.

DVDS TO WATCH

"Empires: Holy Warriors"
PBS Home Video, 2005

"Castle"
PBS Home Video, 2006

CASTLE BOOKS

The Medieval World: An Illustrated Atlas
BY JOHN M. THOMPSON
National Geographic, 2010
Richly illustrated maps let you explore the Middle Ages city by city and century by century.

How to be a Medieval Knight
BY FIONA MACDONALD
National Geographic, 2005
Your complete guide to landing the Middle Age's coolest career

The Castle
BY KATHRYN HINDS
Benchmark Books, 2001
An in-depth look at the daily life of every castle character, including lords, ladies, noble children, and servants

Knights & Castles
BY PHILIP STEELE
Kingfisher, 2008
An illustrated guide to castles and the men in shining armor who defended them

CASTLES TO VISIT

Edinburgh Castle
Edinburgh, Scotland

Tower of London
London, England

Guédelon Castle
Burgundy, France

Hearst Castle
San Simeon, CA, USA

BOLDFACE INDICATES ILLUSTRATIONS.

To Paul and Betty Burkhart, who've experienced more history than I have. –CB

Prepared by the Book Division
Nancy Laties Feresten, *Senior Vice President, Editor in Chief, Children's Books*
Jonathan Halling, *Design Director, Books and Children's Publishing*
Jay Sumner, *Director of Photography, Children's Publishing*
Jennifer Emmett, *Editorial Director, Children's Books*
Carl Mehler, *Director of Maps*
R. Gary Colbert, *Production Director*
Jennifer A. Thornton, *Managing Editor*

Staff for This Book
Priyanka Lamichhane, *Project Editor*
Eva Absher, *Art Director*
Lori Epstein, *Senior Illustrations Editor*
Annette Kiesow, *Illustrations Editor*
Erin Mayes, *Designer*
Kate Olesin, *Editorial Assistant*
Kathryn Robbins, *Design Production Assistant*
Hillary Moloney, *Illustrations Assistant*
Grace Hill, *Associate Managing Editor*
Lewis R. Bassford, *Production Manager*
Susan Borke, *Legal and Business Affairs*

Manufacturing and Quality Management
Christopher A. Liedel, *Chief Financial Officer*
Phillip L. Schlosser, *Senior Vice President*
Chris Brown, *Technical Director*
Nicole Elliott, *Manager*
Rachel Faulise, *Manager*
Robert L. Barr, *Manager*

Captions
Page 1: Built in the nineteenth century, Germany's Lichtenstein Castle sits atop the foundation of a much older castle.
Pages 2-3: The island castle of Eilean Donan was originally built to protect Scotland from Vikings.

Since 1888, the National Geographic Society has funded more than 12,000 research, exploration, and preservation projects around the world. The Society receives funds from National Geographic Partners, LLC, funded in part by your purchase. A portion of the proceeds from this book supports this vital work. To learn more, visit natgeo.com/info.

NATIONAL GEOGRAPHIC and Yellow Border Design are trademarks of the National Geographic Society, used under license.

For more information, visit nationalgeographic.com, call 1-877-873-6846, or write to the following address:
National Geographic Partners
1145 17th Street N.W.
Washington, DC 20036-4688 U.S.A.

Visit us online at nationalgeographic.com/books

For librarians and teachers: ngchildrensbooks.org

More for kids from National Geographic: natgeokids.com

For information about special discounts for bulk purchases, please contact National Geographic Books Special Sales: specialsales@natgeo.com

For rights or permissions inquiries, please contact National Geographic Books Subsidiary Rights: bookrights@natgeo.com

Library of Congress Cataloging-in-Publication Data
Boyer, Crispin.
National Geographic Kids everything castles : capture these facts, photos, and fun to be king of the castle! / by Crispin Boyer. — 1st ed.
    p. cm.
Includes bibliographical references and index.
ISBN 978-1-4263-0803-1 (hardcover : alk. paper) —
ISBN 978-1-4263-0804-8 (library binding : alk. paper)
1. Castles—Juvenile literature. 2. Civilization, Medieval—Juvenile literature. I. Title. II. Title: Everything castles.
GT3550.B69 2011
940.1—dc22
                                                2010026962
Printed in Malaysia
21/IVM/6 (Paperback)
21/IVM/4 (RLB)